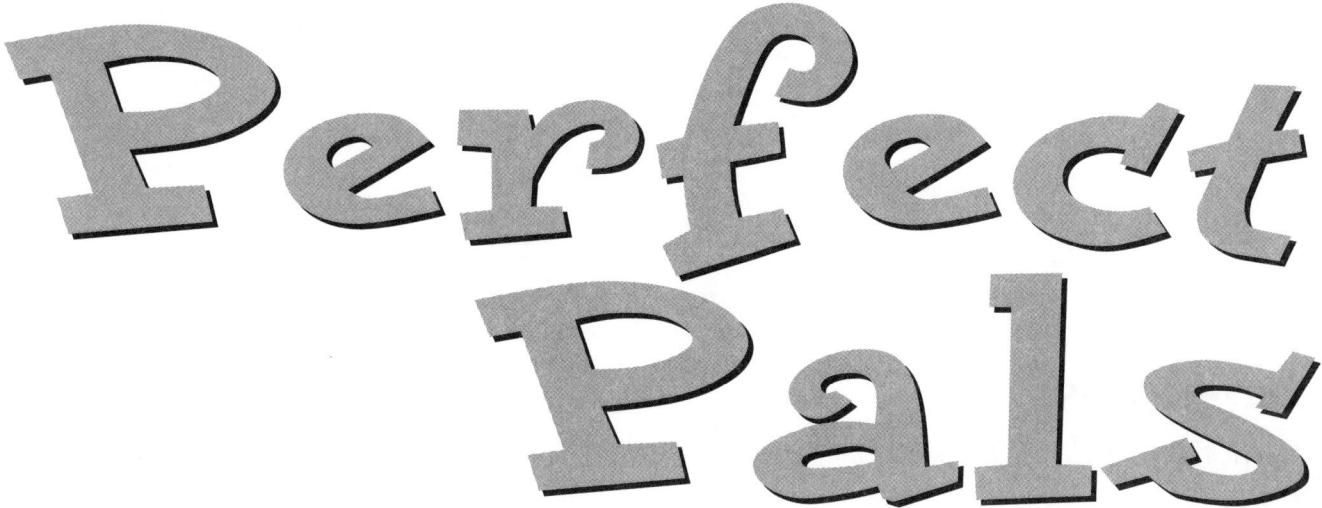

How to Juggle Your Way From Perfection to Excellence

Grades 3-6

Story, Discussion Guide and Student Activities
Janet M. Bender & Amy R. Murray

Perfect Pals
How to Juggle Your Way From Perfection to Excellence
$19.95
ISBN 1-931636-26-5

Copyright 2003 National Center for Youth Issues, Chattanooga, TN

All rights reserved. No part of this publication may be reproduced, stored in a retrieval system or transmitted in any form by any means, electronic, mechanical, photocopy, recording or otherwise without prior written permission from the publisher except for pages 9-19 and 50-71.

Written by:	Janet M. Bender and Amy R. Murray
Cover Design and Layout by Contract:	Tonya Daugherty
Contract Illustrator:	Tonya Daugherty

Published by:

National Center for Youth Issues

National Center for Youth Issues
P.O. Box 22185
Chattanooga, Tennessee 37422-2185
1-800-477-8277
www.ncyi.org

Printed in the United States of America

TABLE OF CONTENTS

About the Authors 4
Dedication / Acknowledgements 5
Introductions by Janet and Amy 6

Background Research
    Why is This Resource Needed? 8
    What Do We Know About Perfectionism? 9
    Are You a Perfectionist? 10
    What Are the Effects of Perfectionism? (chart) 11
    How Can Parents and Teachers Help? 12
    Parent Articles 13
    Excellence VS Perfection (chart) 20

Perfect Pals Storybook 21
    Facilitator Discussion Guide for story 47
    A Little Imperfection (poem) 48

Student Activities / Reproducible Worksheets 49
    "You Might Be a Perfectionist If…" 50
    "Let's Get Real! Is Perfection Possible?" 51
    "Setting Realistic Goals" 52
    "Recognize Steps of Progress Toward a Goal" 53
    "Mistakes are OK" 54
    "Famous Failures" 55
    "Zap Negative Thoughts!" 56
    "Fly High With Uplifting Thoughts" 57
    "Stressed Inside" 59
    "10 Ways to Stay Stress Free" (2 pages) 60
    "Learn to Relax" 62
    "Balancing Work, Play and Rest" 63
    "Trying New Things Can Be Fun" 64
    "Trying New Things" 65
    "Celebrate Accomplishments! Yours and Others" 66
    "Celebrate Success" (group activity) 67
    "Proud to Be Me!" 69
    "Learn to Juggle" 70
    Juggling Directions Diagram 71

Resources and References on Perfectionism 72

About the Authors

Janet Bender is a veteran author, presenter and consultant in the field of elementary counseling. She recently retired after 30 years combined experience as an elementary teacher and school counselor in South Carolina. Her previously published resources include *Ready, Set, Go! A Practical Resource for Elementary Counselors, School Counselor's Scrapbook, My Daddy is in Jail,* and *Easy As Pie... A Generous Serving of Creative Guidance Presentations.*

Amy Murray is currently an elementary school counselor in Dorchester District Two in Summerville, SC. This is her twentieth year in the school system, having worked as both an elementary school teacher and counselor. Amy earned her B.A. degree in elementary education from Clemson University, and her M.Ed. in elementary counseling from The Citadel. Perfect Pals is her first publication.

DEDICATION

To our somewhat perfectionist daughters
Amy and Rachel who offered their insight and advice.

ACKNOWLEDGEMENTS

With Special Thanks:

To Nancy Reed and Robert Rabon and other staff of
National Center for Youth Issues, our publishers, editors and encouragers.

To our husbands Frank and Steve for their patience and support.

INTRODUCTIONS

The idea for this book arose from a conversation I had with a school counselor who was looking for resources to help her work with perfectionist students. I couldn't recall seeing any elementary resources on that topic to recommend to her. Quite frankly, I wasn't even aware of a need for such a resource. After some thought and a little research, I decided to ask a "perfectionist" counselor friend of mine if she would be interested in co-authoring a book with me on the topic.

A few days later as I was having lunch with my adult daughter Amy, I said to her, "I'm thinking about writing a book on perfectionism, but I really don't know much about it." She looked at me with shock and disbelief and said, "You're kidding, right?" In her eyes, I knew a lot about perfectionism from personal experience. That conversation was the beginning of this resource.

I knew that my daughter had perfectionist tendencies, but I attributed it to her giftedness. I never considered myself to be a perfectionist because I don't DO everything perfectly. I just have high standards for myself and for others. As I began to read and research the topic, I learned that many of us have tendencies toward perfectionist thinking. I discovered that perfectionism taken to excess may lead to numerous mental, emotional, physical and relational issues and problems. At age 54, I now consider myself a "recovering perfectionist," grateful that my thinking did not lead to serious problems, and hopeful that this resource can help others make lasting changes from perfectionism to excellence that will result in a happier, healthier future.

Janet M. Bender

I have known Janet for twenty years. When I first became an elementary counselor, Janet had some years of experience and I always looked to her for advice. I admired Janet's work as a counselor and an author, and secretly thought that it would be wonderful to co-author a book with her one day. So, when Janet called me to ask if I would write a book on perfectionism with her, I quickly agreed!

Then I thought—perfectionism. What have I gotten myself into? I have struggled with perfectionism some throughout my life. Many times expecting more of myself, even when I knew I had done my best. In raising my daughter, Rachel, I had consciously tried to prevent her from developing perfectionist thinking. My mind was drawn back to the day, however, when Rachel stated, "I told my Algebra teacher I had to get a 100!" I had been shocked. Rachel had an 'A' average in Algebra 2. Where did this come from? I had always been sure to notice her accomplishments, and compliment her for effort—not perfection.

Next I thought—Do we really need a resource to help counselors work with perfectionist students? The question was answered sooner than I expected as I counseled with students. A third grade girl cried in my office after receiving her report card. She had made a 'C' in Reading. She said, "I know I did my best, but my mom says that 'C's aren't allowed in our house." A learning-disabled third grade boy was upset over learning to write in cursive. He could not make the cursive letters look like his teacher's model, so he refused to try. I found that many students develop perfectionist qualities as they strive to excel in school. I hope that this book will enable counselors to help students make the change from expecting perfection to accepting their best!

Amy R. Murray

Why Is This Resource Needed?

Until recently, I never thought of perfectionism as a problem. In fact, I admired the trait in others, and aspired to achieve perfection in many areas of my own life.

After researching the topic and reflecting on the dynamics of perfectionist thinking in my life and the lives of my students, I began to see things differently.

Instead of viewing "perfection" as an admirable condition devoid of flaws or weaknesses, I now realize that "perfection" is an unattainable standard which, when pursued to excess, may result in negative emotional and relational consequences.

Realistically, we live in a highly competitive society where people often equate self-worth with performance. From an early age, children learn that making A's and winning trophies or contests earns them approval from adults and popularity among their peers.

If a child's quest for achievement is driven primarily by the fear of failure or a strong need for approval and acceptance, it may indicate the presence of some degree of perfectionism.

Perfectionists often set unrealistically high goals for themselves. While others view them as successful, they rarely see their own performance as good enough. This mindset may result in a child who is anxious and hypercritical, or one who is overly competitive, boastful and judgmental. Some perfectionists who fear failure become procrastinating underachievers rather than risk doing a task imperfectly.

In any case, identifying and challenging irrational perfectionist thinking early in a child's life can help him/her move from the frustrating pursuit of the impossible, toward the fulfilling achievement of excellence.

Janet M. Bender

Perfect Pals published by National Center for Youth Issues, Chattanooga, TN.

What Do We Know About Perfectionism?

From several sources we know that perfectionism taken to its extreme can lead to severe physical, emotional and relational problems. Specifically, eating disorders, depression, substance abuse, personality disorders, loss of self-control, chronic anxiety, and other associated illnesses are some of the debilitating effects of excessive perfectionism.

More commonly, individuals exhibiting a moderate degree of perfectionist tendencies often cope with difficulties such as procrastination, low self-esteem, over-commitment, inability to relax, indecisiveness, rigid thinking, and/or chronic anxiety.

Perfectionism is not an "all or nothing" condition. Because perfectionist tendencies exist on a continuum, it is difficult to measure how prevalent it is among the general population. Pyryt (1994) suggests that researchers have identified as many as six dimensions of perfectionism. Hewitt and Flett (1991) developed an instrument, which measures perfectionist thinking in three primary dimensions:

1. Self-Oriented Perfectionism:
   Excessively high standards for oneself

2. Socially-Prescribed Perfectionism:
   Preoccupation with perceptions and expectations of others

3. Other-Oriented Perfectionism:
   Extremely high expectations for others

Educators have expressed concerns about the negative impacts of perfectionism on students, especially the gifted. Their schoolwork, recreational activities and their relationships with others may suffer the side effects of perfectionist thinking (Addecholdt and Goldberg, 1999). Pyryt (1994) cites a Whitmore (1980) study which links perfectionism to underachievement and emotional stress in gifted individuals. Because they do not submit work that is less than perfect, they may become underachievers who feel worthless for failing to live up to unrealistic expectations. There is even some evidence placing perfectionist gifted students at-risk for suicide (DeLisle, 1986).

In summary, research seems to support the conclusion that perfectionism will not lead to the freedom and satisfaction of a balanced life. Trading perfectionism for the pursuit of excellence can lead, ironically, to more "perfect" moments of freedom from guilt, compulsions, frustration, and unnecessary anguish (Stoddard, 1995).

Perfect Pals published by National Center for Youth Issues, Chattanooga, TN.

Are You a Perfectionist?

In a society devoted to perfection, with TV and other media constantly promoting unrealistic fantasies, most of us have at least some areas where we fall prey to perfectionist thinking. As stated earlier, a moderate degree of perfectionist thoughts and actions can be channeled toward a healthy pursuit of excellence. The resources cited at the end of this book contain checklists/assessments for those who want a more formal assessment of your perfectionism. The list provided here may be used as a beginning for increased self-awareness.

Perfectionist Thinking

- ❏ I'd rather do it myself because others might not do it correctly.
- ❏ I can't get started until/unless my desk is perfectly organized.
- ❏ I feel guilty taking time to play or rest, when I have work to do.
- ❏ When I make a mistake, I have a hard time letting it go.
- ❏ Even if I accidentally do something wrong, I have trouble forgiving myself.
- ❏ I don't like asking for or accepting help from others.
- ❏ I would feel very uncomfortable for the rest of the day if I dripped mustard on my shirt at lunch.
- ❏ I often think about what I should have done differently.
- ❏ My life is usually highly organized and scheduled in advance.
- ❏ I become critical of others who don't live up to my standards.
- ❏ I do things I don't really want to do so I won't disappoint anyone.
- ❏ When I play a sport, I can only have fun if I win.
- ❏ I worry a lot about what others will think of me.
- ❏ I feel jealous or angry if others outperform me.
- ❏ I often compare my performance to others.
- ❏ I put off doing things because I'm afraid of making mistakes.
- ❏ I feel stressed out much of the time.

Perfect Pals published by National Center for Youth Issues, Chattanooga, TN.

What Are the Effects of Perfectionism?

MENTAL
- Procrastination
- Underachievement
- Self-criticism
- Anxiety/guilt
- Moodiness
- Over-commitment
- Workaholic/task overload
- Laziness
- Obsessed with winning
- Extremely independent
- Overly responsible

PHYSICAL
- Stress-related symptoms
- Gastrointestinal ailments
- Headaches
- Cardiovascular problems
- Rapid breathing
- Exhaustion
- Insomnia
- Nervous jitters
- Eating disorders
- Difficulty relaxing

EMOTIONAL
- Feelings of worthlessness
- Excessive need for control
- Fear of failure/making mistakes
- Self-mutilation/harm
- Obsessive compulsive tendencies
- Fears/phobias
- At risk for suicide

RELATIONAL
- Overly critical of self/others
- Poor communication skills
- Unforgiving
- Attracted to people with superficial characteristics
- Avoid intimacy
- Sacrifice relationships for activities
- Difficulty complimenting others
- Too busy for fun
- Parental pressure
- Competitive with siblings
- People pleaser

Do these seem "perfect" to you?

How Can Parents and Teachers Help?

1. Listen and take student's concerns seriously.
2. Empathize with student's feelings of frustration.
3. Help student devise a plan to reduce perfectionist thinking. (Don't expect to eliminate it completely.)
4. Recognize and reinforce student's desires to aim high and do their best.
5. Help student restructure goals to be realistic and productive rather than rigid and compulsive.
6. Express and model the expectation that mistakes are a normal part of the learning process.
7. Help student divide assignments into small steps within a larger objective.
8. Build and maintain a friendly, supportive relaxed learning environment.
9. Stress improvement over perfect performance.
10. Explain the harmful effects and possible consequences of perfectionist thinking.
11. Provide an inviting learning environment rather than a rigid authoritarian one.
12. Reassure students that they will get help as needed to achieve success.
13. Communicate approval of student's progress toward a goal.
14. Encourage class participation and reinforce effort and divergent thinking.
15. Praise the child more for his/her positive character qualities than for specific accomplishments.
16. Arrange for professional counseling if needed.

Avoid These Ineffective Strategies

1. Criticizing and nagging.
2. Threatening punishment for failure to change.
3. Trying to control or suppress perfectionist tendencies.
4. Ignoring or denying the problem.
5. Emphasizing the end product more than the process.

For More Information

Brophy, J., and M. Rohrkemper (1989). Teachers' Strategies for Coping with Perfectionist Students. Research Series No. 198. East Lansing, MI: Institute for Research on Teaching, Michigan State University. ED 314 401

Adapted from ERIC digest from: Brophy, Jere (1996). Teaching problem students. New York, NY: Guilford.

Help Your Child Develop Successful Social Skills

Most experts agree that children driven by perfectionist thinking often develop their intellect while remaining deficient in the social arena. Excessive praise and reinforcement for specific accomplishments and intellectual achievements may result in a child with an attitude of superiority or inferiority. Either of these extremes may lead to unpopular behaviors such as bragging, criticizing, ignoring, avoiding or ostracizing others.

Successful social relations foster healthy self-esteem, and self esteem is enhanced by social relations. (Patten, 1999). Encourage your child to play games with other children that require interaction and cooperation. Puppet play, jigsaw puzzles and cooking projects are fun activities that provide natural opportunities to build social skills (Fad, Ross, & Boston, 1995). Cooperative team sports and projects that emphasize the process not the end product can also help.

Teach your child how bragging and criticism impacts others and when criticism is necessary, how to do it sensitively and constructively (Rimm, 1994). The child who learns to consider the feelings and opinions of others will be on the road to success in relationships.

Be a model of healthy excellence. Congratulate yourself when you've done a good job and give others credit when it is due. Try to avoid being overly critical of yourself or others. Your child is likely to model your attitude and behavior.

Developing social skills takes time and practice. Encourage your child to take time to develop friendships. They will bear fruit long after the trophies and report cards are forgotten.

Perfect Pals published by National Center for Youth Issues, Chattanooga, TN.

Help Your Child Learn to Try New Things

We all want our children to be successful. Sometimes parents have such a strong desire for their children to be successful, that they develop expectations so high their children can't reach them. These parents have a low tolerance for mistakes and expect perfection from their children and from themselves. Their children may become frustrated, discouraged or anxious and avoid attempting any new task where there is a possibility of failure or disappointing their parents.

Parents can help by encouraging their children to have fun while learning new things. Children will probably become more successful if they have a healthy attitude toward making mistakes. Teach them that the mistakes they make along the way are learning opportunities. Avoid making every new activity goal oriented. Model a healthy sense of humor when you have difficulty learning something new.

Have fun participating in some of the following activities with your children. You will be teaching academic skills, nurturing your relationships, and helping them develop a healthy attitude toward learning. Remember that it's okay to laugh at your mistakes too!

1. Before taking a trip, read some books or go online to learn about the places you plan to visit.

2. Plan a trip together—decide the places you want to visit and activities you want to pursue.

3. Try cooking a new recipe together.

4. When shopping, compare costs, discounts, and have children practice making change.

5. Sort laundry or grocery items to learn classification skills.

6. Design your own birthday or thank you cards to mail to friends.

7. Record information from billboards as you travel in your car.

8. Learn how to roller blade, juggle, or play a sport together.

Perfect Pals published by National Center for Youth Issues, Chattanooga, TN.

Help Your Child Realize That Mistakes Are Okay

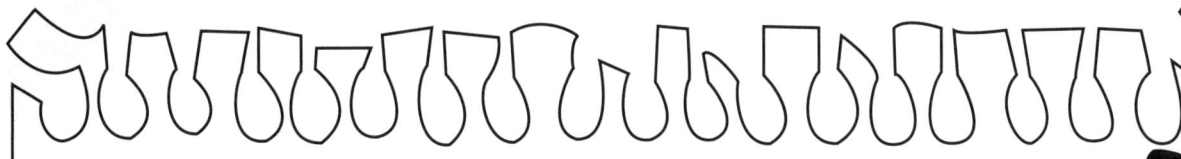

Some children are underachievers; some are overachievers. Underachieving children do not perform as well academically as their potential indicates they can. Overachieving children are constantly working; never completely happy with the end result. What do these children have in common? Perfectionism!

Both underachievers and overachievers feel that mistakes are bad. Underachievers often times are afraid to try new things for fear of making mistakes. They may only attempt activities in which they can easily be successful. Overachievers work constantly to get everything right, in order to avoid making mistakes or getting something wrong. Sometimes they develop unrealistic expectations, believing they can accomplish something when they don't have the talent or ability that's necessary.

Do you find that you have perfectionist qualities? Are you an underachiever or overachiever? Perfectionists don't tolerate mistakes in themselves or their children (Dinkmeyer, McKay, & Dinkmeyer, 1997). Anything less than perfect is considered bad.

Perfectionists can learn to admit their mistakes. Remind yourself and your children that mistakes are not the end of the world. In fact, mistakes can be good! Often each time we make a mistake, we learn something new.

Perfectionists can learn to focus on their efforts and improvements, as well as those of their children. Forget past mistakes; focus on what you and your child have learned to do right. Notice each step that is made toward a desired goal.

Perfectionists can learn to laugh at their mistakes. Aren't mistakes humorous sometimes? Mistakes are not as painful once we learn to laugh at ourselves. Try to chuckle at yourself when mistakes are made. Your children will be watching!

Points of Excellence for Parents

Perfect Pals published by National Center for Youth Issues, Chattanooga, TN.

Help Your Child Learn to Celebrate Accomplishments

In order for children to believe in themselves, they must have parents who believe in them. Parents often give their children praise and approval when they win awards or make A's. The subtle message sent to the child is, "I only matter when I am the best!" The child's self-esteem becomes tied to winning and getting A's. Perfectionist thinking may develop, and the child's anxiety increases as he finds that it's impossible to win at everything!

We want our children to appreciate their own talents, to feel capable, and to feel worthwhile just the way they are (Dinkmeyer, McKay & Dinkmeyer). Children will develop this appreciation for self, even with all their flaws, when encouragement is given. Encouragement notices effort, improvement, and each step taken toward accomplishing a goal. Encouragement can be given when a child is not doing well. Encouragement will give the child the strength to continue trying when it's hard to learn something new.

Offer encouraging statements, such as:
- "You really studied hard for that test."
- "Look at the progress you've made."
- "I can tell you are pleased with the project."
- "You are very good at _____."
- "You're getting better at _____ everyday."
- "I believe you can do it."
- "It looks like you really worked hard on that."
- "It was thoughtful of you to _____."

Although we usually encourage with words, our body language can also offer encouragement. A wink, a smile, a hug, or a pat-on-the-back are other ways to offer encouragement. Acknowledge and celebrate small steps toward a goal.

Let your children know that you have confidence in them through your words and your actions!

Perfect Pals published by National Center for Youth Issues, Chattanooga, TN.

Help Your Child Manage Stress

Signs and symptoms of stress occur in varying degrees among children. A child's personality, genetic make up, and environment all play a part in determining that child's reaction to stressful circumstances. Perfectionists tend to have higher levels of stress because of their unrealistic expectations for themselves. Some of the more common symptoms of stress are listed below.

Emotional	*Mental*	*Physical*
Fear, sadness, irritability, worry, low self-esteem	trouble concentrating, self-criticism, poor decision-making, careless mistakes	Headaches, stomach aches, nausea, sweaty hands, rapid pulse
Behavioral		*Relational*
nail biting, crying, nervous mannerisms, acting out, withdrawal		extreme shyness, withdrawal, teasing, bullying, change in normal behavior

Some children internalize their stress and become withdrawn; others let it out and become aggressive. Parents should watch for a change from the child's normal behavior. To help your child cope with stress, try these ideas.

❑ Ask open-ended questions and listen without criticism. "How are things going with your teacher?"
❑ Give back rubs, hugs and other affectionate touches.
❑ Encourage healthy eating and physical exercise.
❑ Develop fun family activities.
❑ Encourage hobbies.
❑ Be clear, consistent and calm with discipline.
❑ Teach and model relaxation skills.
❑ Provide opportunities to practice problem solving.

Be aware of these common sources of stress.

1. Being away from home / separation from parent
2. Fear of punishment
3. Worry about getting along with peers
4. Worry about school performance
5. Fear of not fitting in
6. Divorce or separation of parents
7. Moving (new town or school)
8. Repeating a grade in school
9. Serious illness (child or family member)
10. Death of close friend or relative
11. Parent deployed to war

Stress is an unavoidable part of life. How you handle it makes all the difference. Be a role model for your children in handling your own stress in a healthy way.

*Adapted in part from Helping children manage stress, Iowa State University, University Extension paper, 1996.

Perfect Pals published by National Center for Youth Issues, Chattanooga, TN.

Help Your Child Set Realistic Goals

Goal setting and the attainment of those goals are ongoing lifelong processes. Like an inchworm, your child will meet with success if he/she learns to tackle life one small step at a time. The earlier a child begins to discern the difference between wishful thinking and realistic goals, the less frustrated he/she will become with him/herself and others. Perfectionist thinkers tend to set rigid and unrealistically high goals for themselves. They may spend too much time trying to do things perfectly or they may procrastinate about getting started for fear of failure.

You can help by maintaining realistic expectations that are consistent with your child's age and capabilities. Try to avoid lavishing your child with praise. Surprisingly, too much praise can put a child on a pedestal where he/she worries about "falling off" and disappointing parents. Let your children know that you don't expect perfection, just their best effort. Perfectionists often believe that the love and approval of parents depends on their perfect performance.

Help your child break tasks into manageable pieces that can be accomplished successfully, and offer encouragement and recognition for progress toward a goal. Discourage competition with others in favor of self-improvement.

When helping your child set realistic goals, check to see if the goal meets these five criteria.

1. Is the goal concrete / measurable?

2. Is the goal specific / detailed?

3. Does the goal state an expected, but flexible time limit?

4. Is the goal attainable, separate from anyone else's actions?

5. Is the goal consistent with your experience and abilities?

Remember that the best lessons for children are those they model from their parents. Do a reality check on your goal setting skills and attitudes. Are you too hard on yourself? Admit your own imperfections without guilt, blame or self-deprecation. You'll score winning points in your child's eyes.

Points of Excellence for Parents

Perfect Pals published by National Center for Youth Issues, Chattanooga, TN.

Help Your Child Have Healthy Self-Esteem

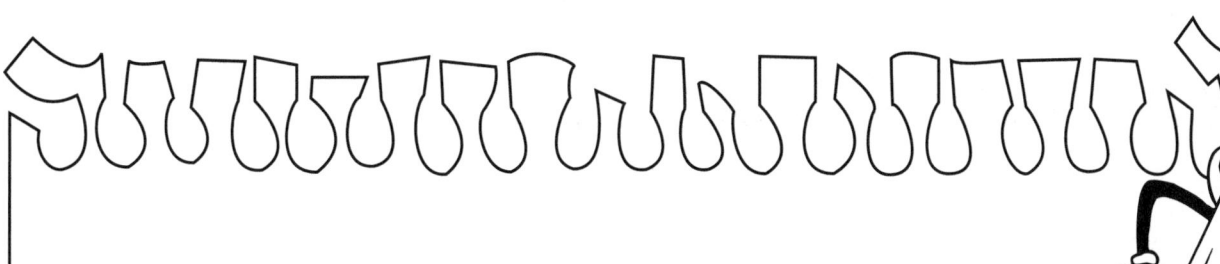

Children know what makes them feel successful and good about themselves. Here's what they say:

➤ *Smile* when you see me.

➤ *Listen* to me when I talk.

➤ Let me know that you *missed* me when you were away.

➤ Recognize my own *special talents*, even if they do not show up on my report card.

➤ Give me a chance to *succeed* in at least one small way each day.

➤ *Praise* me when I do something right.

➤ If you do not like something that I do, help me *understand* that you still like me as a person.

➤ Show me that I have a lot of *options* for the future, and that I can set my own goals.

➤ *Encourage* me to aim high.

➤ Tell me that you *love* me just the way I am!

Source unknown

Perfect Pals published by National Center for Youth Issues, Chattanooga, TN.

When Your Goal Is...

Excellence...   Perfection...

Excellence		Perfection
Achieving steps toward a goal.	YOU FOCUS ON...	Setting and achieving unrealistically high goals.
Joy and challenge of achieving a goal.	YOU ARE MOTIVATED BY...	Fear of failure or disapproval.
Personal satisfaction from good performance; can share in joy of the accomplishments of others.	YOU FEEL...	Inadequate if less than perfect; envious of others and diminished by their success.
An accumulation of previous accomplishments.	YOUR SELF-ESTEEM IS BASED ON...	Each perfect personal performance or accomplishment.
Able to celebrate accomplishments, enjoy tasks for entertainment value. Good sport.	YOUR ATTITUDE TOWARD TASKS, SPORTS, and PLAY IS...	"I'm never good enough," always competitive, poor loser, often angry and depressed if not successful.
Modesty and humility	YOUR RELATIONSHIPS WITH OTHERS MAY DEMONSTRATE...	Boasting, criticism of others.

*Adapted from: Hendlin, Steven J. When Good Enough Is Never Enough: Escaping the Perfection Trap. 1992. G.P. Putnam's Sons. New York, NY.

Perfect Pals published by National Center for Youth Issues, Chattanooga, TN.

Perfect Pals Storybook

Patty heard an odd scraping sound as she worked on an essay in her fifth grade classroom. Immediately she realized that once again Ryan had used his eraser down to a nub.

As Patty leaned slightly to her right to offer him another pencil, she saw that Ryan had only written two words. What was wrong with him, she thought. Ryan was one of the smartest boys she knew, and this year he was the only student in her class who was also in the gifted program.

"Ryan, here's another pencil," Patty whispered very softly.

"Thanks, Patty," Ryan replied flashing his big white smile.

Perfect Pals published by National Center for Youth Issues, Chattanooga, TN.

"Ryan, are you talking again, instead of working?" said Mrs. Stevens with a glare. Walking over to his desk Mrs. Stevens saw that Ryan had only written a couple of words. "You are one of the smartest students I know. Why aren't you writing your essay?"

"I'm still thinking about what I want to say," Ryan replied glumly. Ryan looked down at his paper. He could not understand why he was a whiz at Math and Science, yet could not get his thoughts down on paper. His parents and teachers didn't understand either. They were always telling him that he was smart and that he could write better if he tried. But, often what he wrote down was not what he wanted to say, so he would erase it and write something else. Soon he knew Mrs. Stevens would call time, and then he would take the paper home and struggle with it most of the night.

That afternoon as they got off the bus, Ryan asked Patty to come to his house to play video games.

"I can't," she replied. "I've got to copy my essay over neatly. I made some mistakes on it."

"Aw, can't you do that later?" Ryan asked.

"I'm afraid not, it might take me awhile," Patty replied. "Don't you need to work on your essay anyway?"

"I was going to finish it later," Ryan stated.

"I'll call you when I finish," offered Patty.

Perfect Pals published by National Center for Youth Issues, Chattanooga, TN.

Turning to walk up her drive, Patty thought about how odd Ryan was. She knew he was smarter than her. He understood Math and Science without studying at all. But, when it came to writing he worked so slowly, and always put off getting the work done. Come to think of it, he always put off any work he had to do. She remembered how last week, he had completed his Science project in just two nights. She had been certain he would receive a failing grade on the project, but he had received a 'B.' Patty, on the other hand, never procrastinated with any assignments.

Patty sat down at the kitchen table and immediately pulled out her essay full of corrections and marks, and began copying it over neatly in pen. Into the second paragraph she skipped a word, so she balled up the paper and started again. Patty wanted to make sure that her paper was the best! She would work for hours to make certain it had no errors and was written neatly in ink. She had decided long ago that she would never turn in a written assignment that was less than perfect.

"You didn't call me yesterday," Ryan said at school the next day.

"I'm sorry…. I didn't finish my essay until after dinner," Patty replied.

"Yeah, I figured," Ryan said with a sigh. Patty drove him nuts, he thought. She studied and worked on schoolwork all the time.

It was report card day at school. On their way out to the bus, Patty said excitedly, "I made the 'A' honor roll."

Patty noticed right away that Ryan did not look pleased. They had known each other since Ryan moved across the street almost two years ago. She had never shared her grades with him before, but today she had been excited. Making the 'A' honor roll was a goal she had worked toward for years.

Perfect Pals published by National Center for Youth Issues, Chattanooga, TN.

"Wow…. good for you," Ryan answered smart aleck. "You finally made all A's—Miss Perfect!"

"Well, you don't have to be so ugly. I've studied and worked hard to get all 'A's," Patty answered.

"I'm 10 times smarter than you! If anyone deserves all A's, it's me!" Ryan stated angrily.

Patty was taken aback. She never really thought that Ryan cared that much about grades. Patty knew most skills came easily to him, but he never spent the amount of time on written work that she did. "I didn't know you cared that much," she said feeling her face getting hot. "You don't spend the amount of time on written assignments that I do, Mr. Lazy!"

"I can't get my thoughts down on paper," Ryan said with a sigh. Then stated with a raised voice, "And… I'm tired of hearing about how hard you work!"

"You don't work as hard as I do," Patty said angrily, yet honestly.

"Of course not! No one tries as hard as you do!" Ryan said mockingly. "Well, I'm sick of hearing how hard you work!" he shouted loudly.

"And I'm sick of hearing you say you'll do the work later!" Patty said and started to stomp off.

"Go ahead, and stomp off," Ryan yelled. "I don't want to talk to you anymore!"

"That's just fine with me!" Patty yelled back before turning her head to walk away.

So, for two weeks Patty and Ryan did not speak to each other. They got on the same bus every morning to go to school, but did not speak. Ryan still sat next to Patty in class, but neither spoke to the other. Sometimes Ryan would give Patty a mean look when she answered questions in class. When the school day was over, they got on the same bus for the ride home, but neither spoke. As they got off the bus, they turned and went their separate ways home without speaking. Sometimes Patty would walk away with her nose stuck up in the air.

Perfect Pals published by National Center for Youth Issues, Chattanooga, TN.

Then, it was the Saturday of Ryan's birthday party. Ryan, of course, had not invited Patty.

"Ryan you really should invite Patty!" his mother said for about the tenth time. "I don't know what happened between you two, but you have been friends for a long time."

Ryan was tired of arguing with his mother about it. "Okay," he said reluctantly. "I'll go ask her now."

Ryan crossed the street, and saw Patty skating in her driveway. When Patty saw him, she stopped. "My mom is having a birthday party for me this afternoon," he humbly said. "Do you want to come? It's at four-thirty."

Patty could not believe that Ryan had just invited her to his birthday party. They had not spoken in weeks. She knew it was a last minute invitation, but all her friends from school were going. So, Patty decided she'd go too even though she and Ryan were still not getting along. The party was across the street at his house, so she could come home anytime she decided to.

Perfect Pals published by National Center for Youth Issues, Chattanooga, TN.

The party turned out to be lots of fun! It was a sunny, warm Spring day, so the party was held outside in Ryan's backyard. After cake and ice-cream, Ryan opened all his gifts. Then the surprises began! First an organ grinder and a monkey played some circus songs. Next, a clown came and blew up balloons while twisting them to magically create a dog, cat, pig, or giraffe.

Jerry the Juggler arrived next, juggling different colored scarves. First he juggled only two scarves at a time. Then three, four, and five scarves were being juggled through the air.

After he juggled scarves, he juggled balls. The children were amazed! The juggler announced that he would teach them to juggle if they liked.

Perfect Pals published by National Center for Youth Issues, Chattanooga, TN.

"I'm sure Patty can master juggling in no time," said Ryan teasingly. "After all, she's Miss Perfect."

Patty was so embarrassed; everybody was looking at her. She felt like going home. Then reconsidering, she thought—I'll show him! It can't be that hard!

The juggler suggested Patty begin with two scarves. Patty tried, and dropped both scarves. Then she tried again, and dropped the scarves again.

"Found something you can't do perfectly?" Ryan taunted.

"Then why don't you try smarty pants," Patty answered holding out both scarves to him.

"Oh, I'm having too much fun watching you!" he said with a laugh.

Patty sighed, "Like always you'd rather not try, than get it wrong."

"Not!" Ryan said while taking the scarves out of Patty's hands.

Jerry the Juggler said, "Let me show you how."

All eyes were on the juggler as he explained, while demonstrating at the same time. "You hold a scarf in each hand. Then you throw the scarf out of your right hand towards the left; then throw the scarf in your left hand towards the right. Then you reach out in front to catch a scarf with your left hand, and the other with your right."

The juggler handed Patty two scarves. She and Ryan tried to copy the juggler's movements. Patty threw both scarves up as instructed, but the first one fell to the ground before she could catch it. Ryan was able to throw both scarves up, and catch the first, but the second scarf hit the ground.

"This is not fun," Ryan stated with aggravation. "I quit!"

Jerry the Juggler replied, "Everybody makes lots of mistakes learning to juggle. It takes time. Watch me again." This time the juggler said, "right-left, left-right, catch, catch," as he demonstrated how to juggle again.

"Oh, I think I can do it!" Ryan said excitedly. He tried again, this time saying out loud, "right-left, left-right, catch, catch." Ryan was successful in juggling the two scarves. "I did it! Come on Patty, you can too!"

Patty tried again repeating, "right-left, left-right, catch, catch." But again the scarf on her left fell to the ground. "I'll never be able to do this!" Patty shouted with frustration.

"Yes, you can," said Jerry the Juggler offering encouragement. "You are already making progress toward your goal of juggling. You are throwing the scarf in your right hand towards the left, and the one in your left hand towards the right. That's a great start! Just try again, and have some fun!"

"Okay," answered Patty reluctantly. Again she tried, "right-left, left-right, catch, catch." This time Patty caught the scarf on her left, only dropping the one on her right.

"That's better, Patty," said Ryan really meaning it. Ryan was trying to juggle three scarves. "Juggling three is ten times harder," he added.

All their friends were watching them now, anxious to soon have a turn of their own.

Patty held the scarves in front of her, one in each hand. "Okay, here goes," she said. "Right-left, left-right, catch, catch." This time Patty barely grabbed the second scarf before it hit the ground. "I did it, I did it!" she cried.

Tip #1:
Set realistic goals! You can learn how to juggle with adequate time and practice.

Tip #2:
Recognize steps of progress toward a goal. Notice each thing you do right as you are practicing juggling.

Tip #3:
Realize making mistakes is okay. Juggling is tricky, everybody makes mistakes.

Tip #4:
It can be fun to try new things. Enjoy learning how to juggle. Juggling is fun, even when you goof up.

Tip #5:
Celebrate accomplishments—yours and others! Be proud of yourself and others when you successfully juggle.

Jerry the Juggler began clapping, and so did everyone else.

"Now, before the rest of you try, you must remember my "Tips for Excellence" to juggle successfully!"

The children had all listened well to Jerry the Juggler explain his "Tips for Excellence." As they attempted to juggle, they realized they had learned valuable tips to help them be successful at many things.

Perfect Pals published by National Center for Youth Issues, Chattanooga, TN.

On Monday morning as Patty and Ryan got on the bus, Patty said, "Hey Ryan, your birthday party was lots of fun! Thanks for inviting me!"

"You're welcome, Patty. I'm glad you came," Ryan said meaning it.

"You know what, Ryan? I've never liked making mistakes."

"Neither have I. I guess that's why I've been so slow writing. I wanted it to be just right!"

Patty laughed and said, "But we sure made mistakes juggling!"

"And it was fun making mistakes!" Ryan replied, and then laughed.

Patty just realized something. "You know, Jerry the Juggler taught us that mistakes are okay."

"And it can be fun to mess up!" Ryan added with excitement.

"Yes, we can't be perfect, but we can always do our best!"

Facilitator Discussion Guide for Perfect Pals

(Questions designated with a (P) are personal ones for student reflection.)

1. Why did it take Ryan so long to write an essay?

2. Why do you think Ryan erased so much?

3. What subjects did Ryan perform well in?

(P) 4. Tell about your best and worst school subjects.

(P) 5. What hobbies or extracurricular activities are easy for you? Which ones are difficult?

6. What does it mean to "procrastinate?"

7. What are some reasons a person like Ryan might "procrastinate" or put off doing an assignment?

(P) 8. Do you ever put things off? If so, when and why?

9. Do all smart students make good grades? Why or why not?

10. Even though Patty and Ryan were good friends, they were different in some ways. How were they different in their approach to their school assignments?

11. What did Ryan and Patty argue about?

(P) 12. Has teasing or bragging ever caused an argument between you and a friend?

13. What new skill did the children learn at Ryan's birthday party?

14. What frustrated Patty about juggling?

15. What did learning to juggle teach Patty and Ryan about making mistakes?

16. How did Patty feel when she accomplished her goal of learning to juggle two scarves?

(P) 17. Tell about a time when you felt good about learning something new.

Review Jerry the Juggler's Tips for Achieving Excellence:

- Set Realistic Goals
- Mistakes Are OK
- Celebrate Accomplishments— Yours and Others
- Recognize Steps of Progress Toward Your Goal
- Have Fun Trying New Things

A Little Imperfection

By Kathy Schinski

A little imperfection is not so bad.
A little imperfection shouldn't make you feel sad,
It keeps you in touch with reality
And with all the not so perfect people
Just like me.

A little imperfection is not so tough.
You need a little of it to be perfect enough.
It puts your feet back on the earth
And lets the other people keep
Their own self-worth.

A little imperfection in just the perfect place
Can make this not so perfect world easier to face,
More of us could go in the right direction
If we could learn to put up with a little imperfection.

A little imperfection is not so bad.
A little imperfection shouldn't make you feel sad.
It keeps you in touch with reality
And with all the not so perfect people
Just like me.

From: Nelson, Jane. (1987) Positive Discipline. New York, NY: Ballantine Books.

Student Activities

from Perfection to Excellence

Perfect Pals published by National Center for Youth Issues, Chattanooga, TN.

You Might Be a Perfectionist If...

- ❑ You'd rather **do it yourself** because others might not do it correctly.
- ❑ You can't get started until/unless your desk is perfectly **organized**.
- ❑ You feel **guilty** taking time to play or rest, when you have work to do.
- ❑ You have a hard time **letting it go** when you make a mistake.
- ❑ You have trouble **forgiving** yourself, even if you do something wrong by accident.
- ❑ You don't like asking for or accepting **help** from others.
- ❑ You would feel very **uncomfortable** for the rest of the day if you dripped mustard on your shirt at lunch.
- ❑ You often think about what you **should** have done differently.
- ❑ Your life is usually highly **organized** and **scheduled** in advance.
- ❑ You become **critical** of others who don't live up to your standards.
- ❑ You do things you **don't really want** to do so no one will be disappointed in you.
- ❑ You can only have fun if you **win** at sports.
- ❑ You **worry** a lot about what others will think of you.
- ❑ You feel **jealous or angry** if others outperform you.
- ❑ You often **compare** yourself to others.
- ❑ You **put off** doing things because you're afraid of making mistakes.
- ❑ You feel **stressed** out much of the time.

How many did you check? _____

What did you learn about yourself?

_____

_____

_____

LET'S GET REAL!
Is Perfection Possible?

Perfection is defined as: *"complete in all respects; flawless."* We know that all living things grow and change from day to day.

Is it possible for a growing, changing person to be *"complete in every way"*?

Is it possible for anyone to be perfect? Why or why not?

Excellence means: *"superior; unusually good."*

Is it possible for a living, growing person to be *"superior or unusually good"*?

Is it possible for a person to be excellent in some things? Why or why not?

When you try to be perfect, you may feel unhappy or nervous much of the time because you are trying to do the impossible. When setting goals for yourself, always try to choose goals that are possible for you to reach.

Think about the following goals/thoughts. Mark **P** or **E** to show whether these thoughts come from a person striving for **P**erfection or **E**xcellence. It will help to imagine the feelings that go with each thought.

1. ____ I must get this right, or the teacher will be disappointed in me.
2. ____ I'll feel good if I do better this week on my spelling test than I did last week.
3. ____ If I don't get good grades, no one will like me.
4. ____ I have to win this contest so people will notice me.
5. ____ Even though I didn't win today, I tried my best.
6. ____ It's not fair that my sister made all A's.
7. ____ If I make 100%, I can finally stop worrying all the time.
8. ____ I wonder what others are thinking and saying about me.
9. ____ My brother is a good basketball player and I'm good at soccer.
10. ____ I had fun learning something new today.
11. ____ If I can't be the best, I won't even try.

Check yourself.
   Statements #1, 3, 4, 6, 7, 8 and 11 are perfectionist thoughts.
   Statements #2, 5, 9 and 10 are excellent thoughts.

Positive Self-Talk: "I will get real with my expectations for myself and others."

Setting Realistic Goals

We all have things we want to accomplish in life. Suppose you wanted to learn to juggle. Check out these criteria for setting a goal. A realistic goal is:

1. **Concrete:** *"I want to learn to juggle..."*
2. **Specific:** *"...3 scarves"*
3. **Within a set time limit:** *"by the end of this week."*
4. **Attainable separate from anyone else's actions:** *"yes"*
5. **Consistent with your experiences and abilities:** *"yes"*

Think of a **school related goal** you want to reach. Write a realistic goal using the five criteria above. My goal is…

1. _____
2. _____
3. _____
4. _____
5. _____

Check to see if your goal is:
- ❏ Concrete?
- ❏ Specific?
- ❏ Within a set time limit?
- ❏ Attainable separate from anyone else's actions?
- ❏ Consistent with your experiences and abilities?

Think of a **hobby or recreational goal** you want to reach. Write a realistic goal using the five criteria above. My goal is…

1. _____
2. _____
3. _____
4. _____
5. _____

Check to see if your goal is:
- ❏ Concrete?
- ❏ Specific?
- ❏ Within a set time limit?
- ❏ Attainable separate from anyone else's actions?
- ❏ Consistent with your experiences and abilities?

Share your goals with the group.

Positive Self-Talk: *"I can meet my goals if they are realistic."*

Perfect Pals published by National Center for Youth Issues, Chattanooga, TN.

Recognize Steps of Progress toward a Goal

If a task seems overwhelming, it may be because you're seeing only two choices: *right or wrong, good or bad, perfect or not.*

Try breaking it down into smaller steps or parts. Set a goal to complete one step, finish it. Then, start on another small step or task. Give yourself a "pat on the back" for completing each small step.

Dump that **All** or **Nothing** Thinking!

Example:
This room is a mess! I'll never get it all cleaned up.

MESSY ROOM — make bed — *Looking Good Already!* — pick up toys — pick up clothes — *Even Better! Almost Done!* — dust furniture — sweep or vacuum floor — CLEAN ROOM

Think of a job or task that you see as overwhelming. Break it into smaller steps.

Task: _____

Steps to accomplish task: **Check off when complete:**

1 _____ ❏
2 _____ ❏
3 _____ ❏
4 _____ ❏
5 _____ ❏

Remember to give yourself credit for each step you accomplish.

Positive Self-Talk: *"I can achieve my goal one small step at a time."*

Perfect Pals published by National Center for Youth Issues, Chattanooga, TN.

Mistakes Are OK

Sometimes you may see problems or mistakes as larger than they really are. This may result in negative thoughts about yourself or others.

What do you think to yourself when you make a mistake?
_____

What bothers you most about making a mistake?
_____

If you have a tendency to be hard on yourself, try to do these things:
  1. ***Remind yourself that this is an unhealthy habit.***
  2. ***Get feedback from a friend or relative.***
  3. ***List the evidence/facts that support or disprove your negative view of yourself.***

Sometimes you may make less of—minimize—positive things that you accomplish. Take time to list all the little things that went well during the day. It's not bragging to acknowledge your accomplishments to yourself.

> **Examples:**
>   OK: *I got along with my sister. I finished all my chores.*
>   Good: *I improved my spelling grade 5 points.*
>   Great: *I learned to juggle today.*

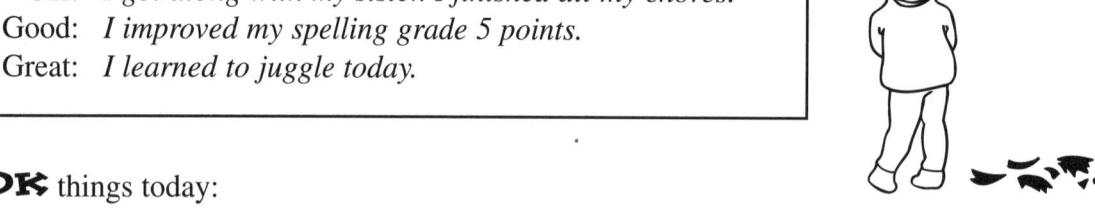

OK things today:
_____
_____

Good things today:
_____
_____

Great things today:
_____
_____

Positive Self-Talk: *" Everyone makes mistakes."*
"Mistakes are a normal part of learning."

Perfect Pals published by National Center for Youth Issues, Chattanooga, TN.

Famous Failures

Did you know?

Almost every successful person has bounced back from failure.

- **Michael Jordan** was cut from his high school basketball team, before becoming the best basketball player ever.

- **Walt Disney** was fired by a newspaper editor because his ideas were bad; then he invented Mickey Mouse.

- **Thomas Edison** was told he was too stupid to learn anything when he was in grade school, before becoming a famous inventor.

- **Winston Churchill** failed the 6th grade; then became Prime Minister of England.

- **Beethoven** once had a music teacher who told him he was hopeless as a composer, before becoming one of our most famous composers.

- **Dr. Seuss** received one hundred rejections before his first book got published. Now he is considered one of the best authors of children's books.

- **Steven Spielberg** was learning disabled and dropped out of high school, before becoming a famous director.

Think of something that you couldn't do when you were five years old, but you can do now. Write or tell how you became successful with it. _____
_____
_____
_____
_____
_____

Positive Self-Talk: *" One poor performance does not equal failure."*

(Hendlin, 1992)

Zap Negative Thoughts!

Do you ever catch yourself thinking thoughts like these?

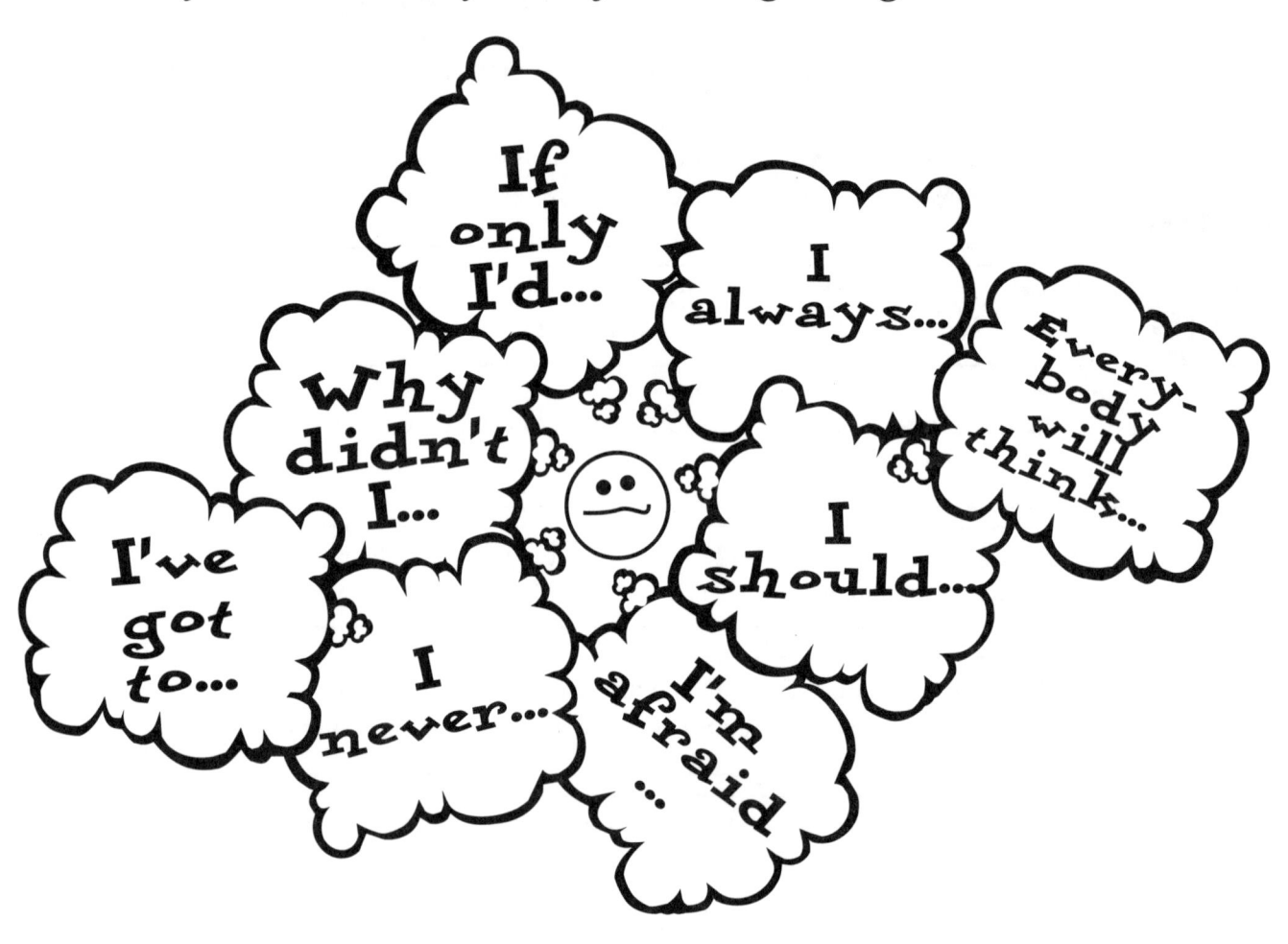

If only I'd...
I always...
Everybody will think...
Why didn't I...
I should...
I've got to...
I never...
I'm afraid...

Try to catch yourself when you think negative thoughts, and re-word the statement into a more positive one. Practice on these:

"If only I'd studied more, I could have made an A instead of a B."

*reworded:*_____

"Everyone will think I'm clumsy since I spilled my lunch tray."

*reworded:*_____

Copy and cut out the uplifting thought cards on the next two pages. Learn one each day. Repeat it to yourself several times. Display each one in a visible place to remind you to think positively.

Positive Self-Talk: *"I'm OK just as I am."*

Perfect Pals published by National Center for Youth Issues, Chattanooga, TN.

Fly High With Uplifting Thoughts

"Perfection is impossible; perfectionism is an imperfection in itself."	"Perfectionism spells paralysis." Winston Churchill
"I am special because there is nobody just like me."	"My value does not depend on winning."
"I will give my best effort in all things."	"One poor performance does not equal failure." Hendlin
"Today, I will be satisfied with 'good' performance."	"I will 'get real' with my expectations for myself and others."
"I am OK just as I am."	"I will 'shake off' my mistakes and move on."
"I will respect myself for seeking excellence not perfection."	"I will balance my time between work, play, and rest."

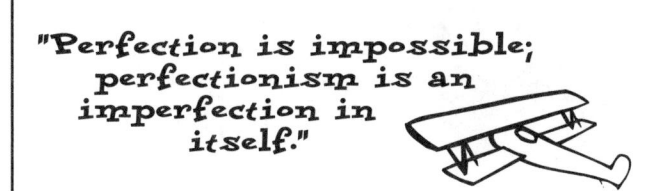

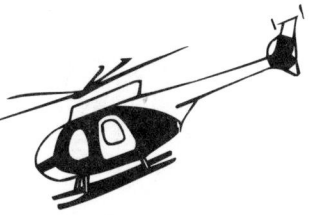

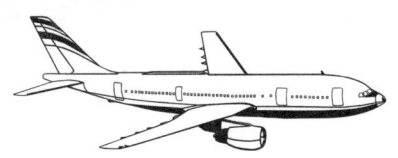

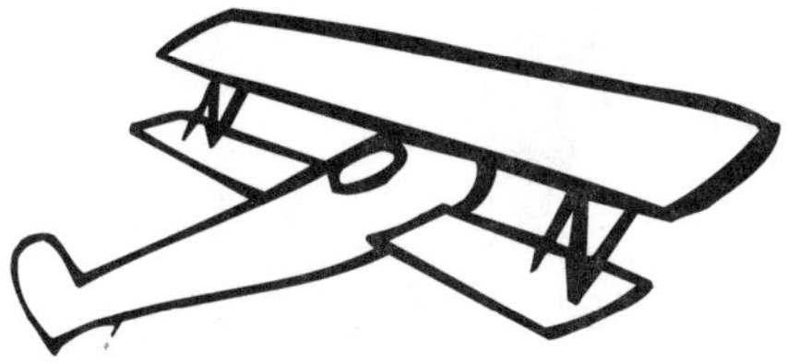

Perfect Pals published by National Center for Youth Issues, Chattanooga, TN.

"I will not allow myself to feel guilty for making mistakes when I have done my best."	"I will appreciate and recognize the accomplishments of others."
"I love and accept myself as I am."	"Today I will celebrate small successes."
"I will think for myself and try to find creative solutions to problems."	"I will only be perfect in my imperfection."
"I can do many things well."	"I will have the courage to try new things."

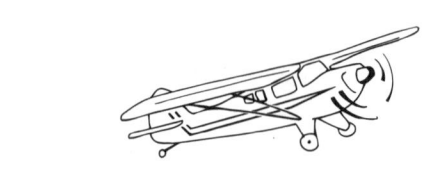

Perfect Pals published by National Center for Youth Issues, Chattanooga, TN.

Perfect on the outside, feeling stressed on the inside?

Perfectionists are hard on themselves. Excellence isn't good enough. Setting unrealistic goals, or having too many goals, often leads to stress.

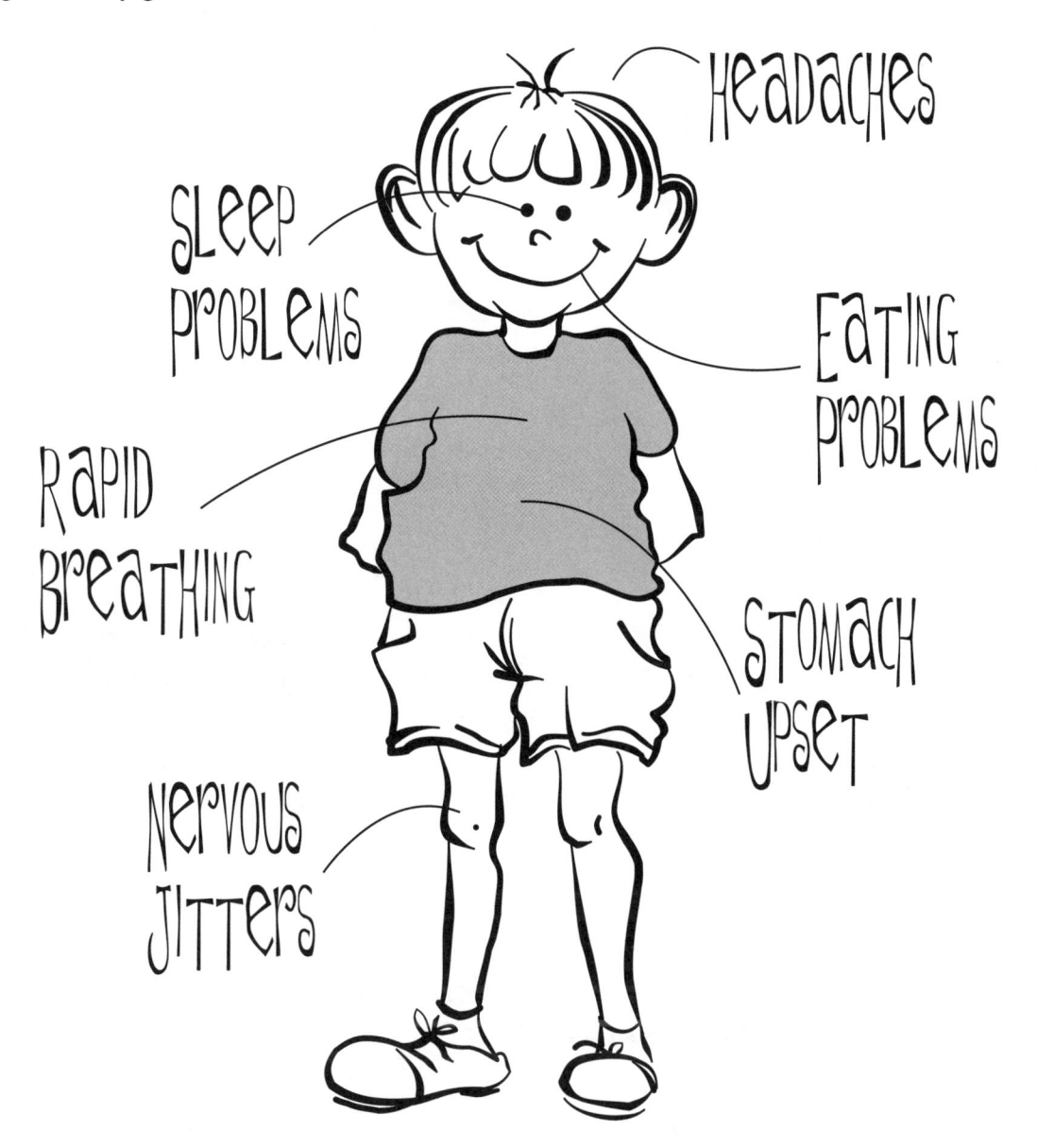

- HEADACHES
- SLEEP PROBLEMS
- EATING PROBLEMS
- RAPID BREATHING
- STOMACH UPSET
- NERVOUS JITTERS

Which of these or other physical symptoms do you experience on a regular basis?

_____

_____

Positive Self-Talk: *"No one can make me feel inferior without my consent."* —Eleanor Roosevelt

Perfect Pals published by National Center for Youth Issues, Chattanooga, TN.

10 Ways to Stay Stress Free

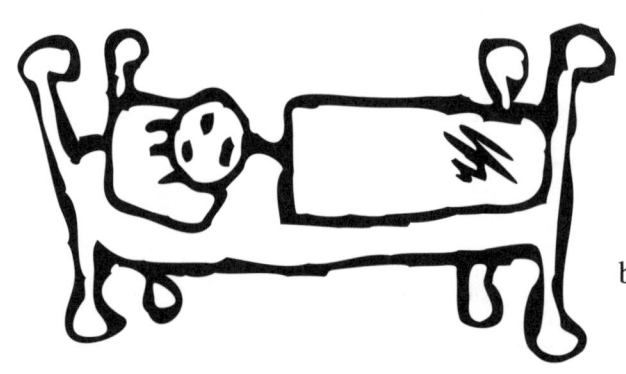

➥ Most importantly: Set realistic goals. Make sure you set goals that are possible for you to achieve, and don't set too many goals.

➥ Notice what you do well. When you've accomplished a goal; be proud of yourself.

➥ Do something physical. Work off tensions by taking a walk or playing a sport.

➥ Eat right! Having adequate nutrition, helps you handle stress.

➥ Get enough sleep. Most children need eight or more hours of sleep each night to be able to do their work well.

Perfect Pals published by National Center for Youth Issues, Chattanooga, TN.

➼ Listen to music. Music is relaxing to most people.

➼ Read a good book. Most people can relax by reading a book they enjoy.

➼ Develop friendships. There is nothing more relaxing than being with friends you enjoy.

➼ Learn to laugh and play. Make sure you have time for hobbies and activities you enjoy.

➼ Talk about problems. When you begin to feel anxious about a situation, talk to a counselor or adult friend.

Positive Self-Talk: *"We deserve the time to play."* —Alexandra Stoddard

Perfect Pals published by National Center for Youth Issues, Chattanooga, TN.

LEARN TO RELAX

Your imagination is a powerful tool in relaxation. Try this process whenever a stressful situation occurs.

1. **Get comfortable and close your eyes.**
2. **Begin to breathe deeply from your diaphragm.**
3. **Imagine yourself doing something relaxing or exciting such as:**

- Resting in a warm, cozy bed on a rainy day
- Sitting in the warm sun at the beach listening to and watching the ocean
- Hitting a perfect shot in your favorite sport
- Enjoying time at your best friend's party

4. **Stretch your arms, take a deep breath, and open your eyes.**

(source unknown)

Positive Self-Talk: *"I will practice relaxation regularly."*

After this exercise, help each student create a relaxing place of their own by asking the following questions:

1. *Where is a place that makes you feel relaxed?*
2. *What are you doing there?*
3. *What's the weather like?*
4. *How do you feel?*

The next time you feel stressed, take a few moments to imagine a visit to your special place.

Perfect Pals published by National Center for Youth Issues, Chattanooga, TN.

Balancing
Work, Play, and Rest

Perfectionists often struggle with maintaining a healthy balance in their lives. Sometimes they spend too much time trying to get work or school projects completed perfectly. This can mean that they feel tired and overloaded. It's important to take time for rest and recreation. Fill in this chart to see how well you're juggling work, play and rest.

Hours Each Week Spent On...

School & School Work								Hobbies, Sports, Fun								Rest & Relaxation							
M	TU	W	TH	F	Sat	Sun	M	TU	W	TH	F	Sat	Sun	M	TU	W	TH	F	Sat	Sun
TOTAL								TOTAL								TOTAL							

There are 168 hours in a week. How well are you doing with balancing your life?
- ❏ Pretty well
- ❏ So-so
- ❏ Way out of balance

If needed, what changes will you make to strive for a better balance?

Positive Self-Talk: *"I will balance my time between work, play, and rest."*

Perfect Pals published by National Center for Youth Issues, Chattanooga, TN.

Trying New Things Can Be Fun

(Teacher/Counselor Directed Activities Individually or in Small Groups)

Scribble Pictures: Usually teachers and parents want students to do their very best work. Just this once, I want you to do whatever you feel like doing when I tell you to start. On this sheet of drawing paper, I want you to make the ugliest picture you can make in one minute. After you finish, tell someone why you think your drawing is the ugliest. Did you have fun? Why? *(Adapted from: Scribble pictures, School Counselor's Scrapbook. (2002) Janet M. Bender. Chapin, SC: Youthlight, Inc.)*

Pound It: Give student a portion of modeling clay or Play Doh®. Using a tape player or other music source, play a sort of musical chairs with this art activity. Start the music. Give students directions to pound, roll, poke, squeeze, stretch or other directives to the clay. They are not to try to make any recognizable object. Stop the music suddenly and have students freeze. Look at "things" they have made. Try to give imaginative names to the blobs as in finding cloud pictures. The goal is to be spontaneous.

Left-Handed Drawing: (Or non-dominant hand) Give oral directions for drawing something that is simple to draw with one's dominant hand. EX: Draw a tree, house, etc. Let student give you directions for the same. Discuss how something can be easy if you have practiced it, but that we all make mistakes when learning something new. Also good for discussing that everyone has different strengths and talents.

Group Juggling: With a small group (4-6) students, and yourself, stand in a circle. Using beanbags, leader begins by calling out one person's name and then tossing a beanbag to that person. That person calls out another name in group and tosses bag to him/her. This continues until the last person returns the beanbag to the leader. Practice this order several times. Ask group if they are ready to try two beanbags. If so, begin the first beanbag. As soon as the receiver has tossed the first bag on to the next person in the circuit, call his/her name and toss the second beanbag. Both bags continue until someone drops one or the leader stops the beanbags. If successful with two, go on to 3 and then 4 adding one at a time. Let the group decide each time if they want the challenge of trying one more. If group fails to "juggle" at least 2 successfully, stop and discuss what went wrong, lessons learned that each person can do to help the group succeed. Juggling is one activity that always begins with mistakes, but ends in lots of fun. *(Adapted from: Bean bag toss. School Counselor's Scrapbook. (2002) Janet M. Bender. Chapin, SC: Youthlight, Inc.)*

Finger Painting: Using finger paint or chocolate pudding on finger paint paper, have students have fun spreading, drawing, erasing and re-drawing designs with their fingers and hands.

Positive Self-Talk: *"It's fun to try new activities."*

Trying New Things

It can be challenging but fun to learn new things. Look at the pictures below. Have you tried any of them? Tell about what you tried. Could you do it well the first time, or did it take some practice? What problems/challenges might have happened while you were learning these things?

Think of something new that you would like to learn. Draw pictures showing what might happen as you learn.

Positive Self-Talk: *"I have the courage to try something new."*

Celebrate Accomplishments!
Yours and Others

Everyone needs a "pat on the back" once in a while. These are some ways you can enjoy your own accomplishments and give others recognition for their positive achievements.

Pat on the Back:
   Actually cut out a hand and wrist print on card stock. Write a complimentary note to a friend and present it to him or her.

Tada!
   Look yourself in the mirror, smile at yourself, and give yourself a "Tada!" for something or for nothing at all.

Drum Roll:
   When a friend has achieved something good, give him/her a drum roll and make a positive announcement of congratulations.

Standing Ovation:
   Same as drum roll, but in a group. Notice when someone needs a little encouragement, and say,"Let's give ___ a standing ovation." Clap enthusiastically.

Badge of Honor:
   Use a badge maker (or ribbon, name tag, etc.) to design a special badge for someone you care about.

Good News Journal:
   Keep a journal or diary of your little daily accomplishments and positive events. Look back over it when you need a "pick me up."

Book Mark:
   Choose a positive, encouraging statement and write it on a bookmark that you use often.

Warm Fuzzy Notes:
   Draw/write notes of encouragement to friends, teachers, parents, and/or siblings.

Positive self-talk: *"Look for the good in others."*

Perfect Pals published by National Center for Youth Issues, Chattanooga, TN.

Celebrate Success

Ask students to define "accomplishment." (something done successfully; social art or skill) Have students brainstorm different accomplishments of theirs and others. List their answers on chart paper or board. Be sure to include social skills as well as more measurable achievements.

Reproduce on paper or card stock a copy of the trophy that follows. Have students write their name on the plaque of the trophy. Seat students in small groups of about four. Students should then exchange trophies among group members and write one skill or accomplishment each person in their group has achieved. Return trophies to owners.

Encourage the children to share one of their accomplishments aloud with the class or group. Discuss their feelings about the positive comments written by other students. Suggest that the children take their trophy home and tape it to their mirror. Each morning after getting dressed, ask them to look into the mirror and read their accomplishments aloud. Remind them that with effort they can continue to reach excellence in many areas.

Positive Self-Talk: *"Today I will celebrate small successes."*

Trophy Handout for "Celebrate Success"

Perfect Pals published by National Center for Youth Issues, Chattanooga, TN.

Proud To Be Me!

I am proud of me because I have these character traits.

- ❏ Responsibility
- ❏ Respect
- ❏ Honesty
- ❏ Compassion
- ❏ Self-discipline
- ❏ Courage
- ❏ Perseverance
- ❏ Citizenship

Choose one of the traits above and tell or write what it means to you.

_____
_____
_____

I am proud of me because I am good at these subjects.

- ❏ Reading
- ❏ Math
- ❏ Science
- ❏ Social Studies
- ❏ Creative Writing
- ❏ Music
- ❏ Art
- ❏ PE
- ❏ Computer

I always try to do my best, but these subjects are difficult for me:

❏ _____   ❏ _____

Positive Self-Talk: "*I will respect myself for seeking excellence, not perfection.*"

Perfect Pals published by National Center for Youth Issues, Chattanooga, TN.

Learn to Juggle

Follow the steps below.
Practice each step before you move on.
Remember Jerry the Juggler's tips.
In time, you can become an excellent juggler.

Steps For Learning To Juggle

1. Start with one scarf. Toss it up with one hand and catch it with the other hand. Repeat back and forth until comfortable.

2. With two scarves, one in each hand, toss up the right one and then follow with the left one in a crisscross motion. Catch the first scarf with your left hand and the second one with your right hand as they float down. Say to yourself, "1, 2, catch, catch." Repeat until comfortable. You can stop here if you choose and pat yourself on the back. If you want to try three scarves, continue.

3. With three scarves, you'll need to hold two scarves in the right hand (one between thumb and forefinger, the other between forefinger and middle finger) and one in the left hand. Using the same crisscross motion, release one of the two scarves first, then the left-handed scarf then back to the remaining scarf in the right hand. You will catch the first scarf with the left hand as soon as the left scarf is released, then continue saying to yourself, "1, 2, 3, 1, 2, 3" as you toss the scarves in the air. Expect to drop scarves and have to start over many times. Keep practicing 5-10 minutes every day until you can keep all three scarves moving through the air.

Directions for Juggling Two Scarves

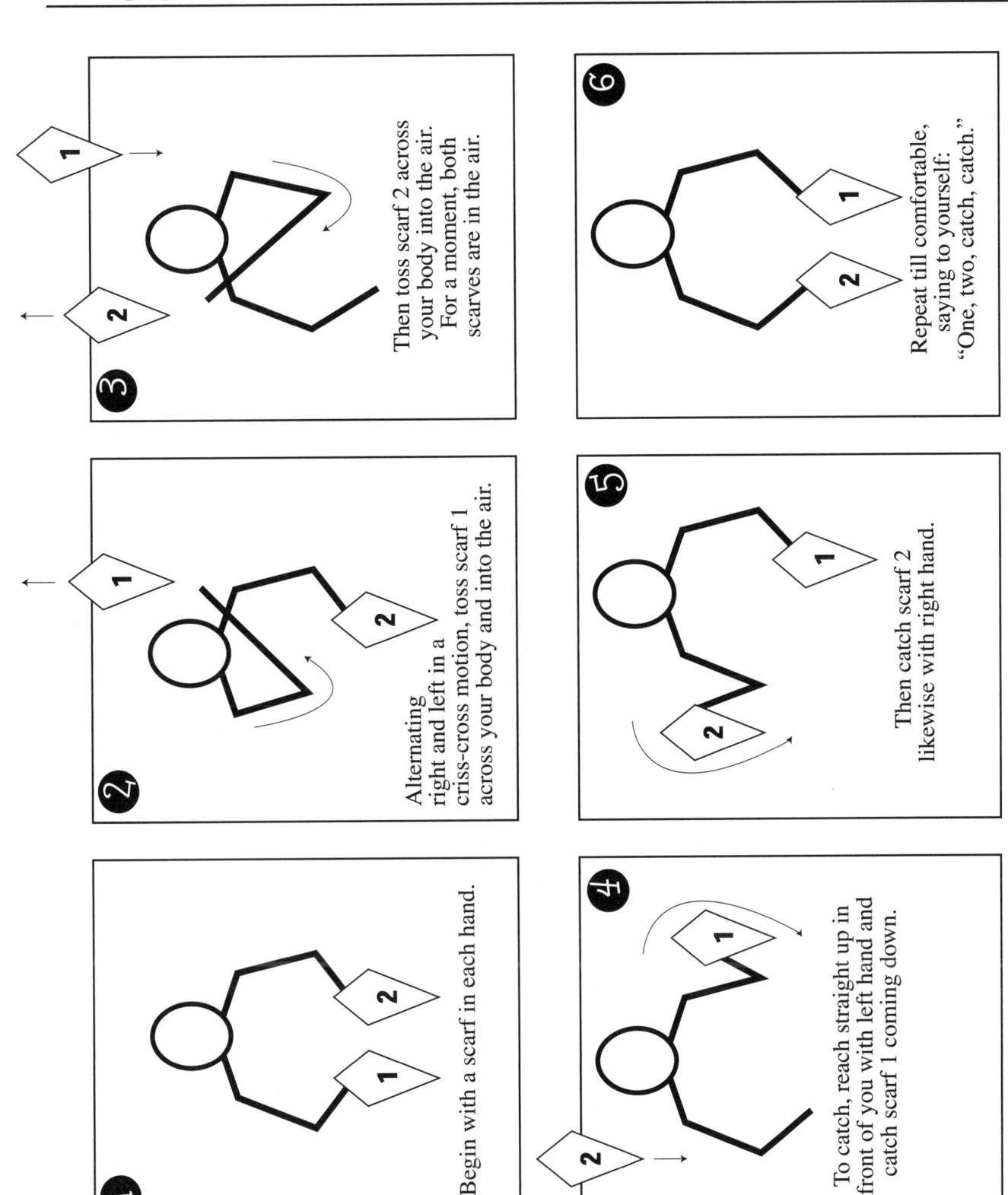

1. Begin with a scarf in each hand.

2. Alternating right and left in a criss-cross motion, toss scarf 1 across your body and into the air.

3. Then toss scarf 2 across your body into the air. For a moment, both scarves are in the air.

4. To catch, reach straight up in front of you with left hand and catch scarf 1 coming down.

5. Then catch scarf 2 likewise with right hand.

6. Repeat till comfortable, saying to yourself: "One, two, catch, catch."

To juggle 3 scarves, use the same criss-cross motion. Begin with scarves 1 & 2 in your right hand and scarf 3 in your left. Alternate tossing right, left, right, catch, catch, catch.

Perfect Pals published by National Center for Youth Issues, Chattanooga, TN.

Resources and References

Adderholdt, Miriam Jan Goldberg (1999). *Perfectionism: What's Bad About Being Too Good?* Minneapolis, MN: Free Spirit Publishing, Inc.

Basco, Monica R. (1999). *Never Good Enough: How to Use Perfectionism to Your Advantage Without Letting it Ruin Your Life.* New York, NY: Touchstone, Simon & Shuster.

Brophy, Jere (1996). *Working with Perfectionist Students.* ERIC Digest adapted from Teaching problem students, New York, NY: Guilford. EDO-PS-96-9.

Dinkmeyer, Don, Sr., Gary D. McKay, and Don Dinkmeyer, Jr.(1997). *The Parent's Handbook, Systematic Training for Effective Parenting.* Circle Pines, MN: American Guidance Services, Inc.

Fad, Kathleen, Melanie Ross, and Judith Boston (1995). *We're Better Together, Teaching Exceptional Children.* Reston, VA: The Council for Exceptional Children.

Finnigan, Dave (1999). *Juggling for Success.* Atlanta, GA: Sportime International.

Hendlin, Steven J. (1992). *When Good Enough is Never Enough: Escaping the Perfection Trap.* New York, NY: G. P. Putnam's Sons.

Molgaard, Virginia (1996). *Helping Children Manage Stress.* University Extension Paper. Ames, IA: Iowa State University.

Patten, Peggy (1999). *Self-esteem: too much of a good thing?* [Article]. Parent News for November-December (Online).

Pyryt, Michael C. (1994). *Perfectionism and Giftedness: Examining the Connection.* Calgary, Alberta: 5th Annual SAGE Conference, University of Calgary.

Rimm, Sylvia B. (1993). *How to Stop Underachievement* [newsletter]. 3(2). Cleveland, OH.

Stoddard, Alexandra (1995). *The Art of the Possible: The Path from Perfectionism to Balance and Freedom.* New York, NY: AVON BOOKS.